THE MYSTERIES OF PURITY

THE

MYSTERIES OF PURITY

Being A Translation With Notes

of

The Kitab Asrar al-Taharah

of

Al-Ghazzali's "Ihya' 'Ulum al-Din"

By

NABIH AMIN FARIS

AMERICAN UNIVERSITY OF BEIRUT

KITAB BHAVAN

New Delhi-110002

Kitab Bhavan
Publishers, Distributers, Exporters & Importers
1784, Kalan Mahal, Darya Ganj
New Delhi-110002 (India)

Phone : (91-11)23277392/93, 23274686
website : www.kitabbhavan.com
e-mail : nasri@vsnl.com

2nd Edition : 2008

ISBN : 81-7151-159-7

Published in India by:
Nusrat Ali Nasri for Kitab Bhavan
1784, Kalan Mahal, Darya Ganj
New Delhi-110002 (India)

Printed in India at:
H.S. Printers
New Delhi-110002

PREFACE

Though one of the most important works coming down to us from Medieval Islam, no single part of the *Ihya' 'Ulum al-Din* appeared in English, or any European language at that, until Duncan B. Macdonald published in the *Journal of the Royal Asiatic Society* (1901, pp. 195-252, 705-748, and 1902, pp. 1-28) an English version of Book VIII of the second quarter of the *Ihya', i.e., the Kitab Adab al-Sama' w-al-Wajd* (On Audition and Grief). The second complete part of the *Ihya'* was Edwin E. Calverley's translation of Book IV of the first quarter, *i.e.*, the *Kitab al-Salah* (Madras, 1925). Except for a few extracts and selections, no complete translation of any part of the *Ihya'* appeared in English until 1962 when two books from it were finally published: Book I of the first quarter, namely, the *Kitab al-'Ilm* (The Book of Knowledge), translated by the present writer and published by M. Ashraf, Lahore, and Book III of the fourth quarter, namely, the *Kitab al-Khawf w-al-Raja* (On Fear and Hope), translated by William McKane and published by Brill of Leiden. The following year, 1963, saw also the publication, in English, of two other books of the *Ihya'*: Book X of the second quarter, on the Conduct of Life as Exemplified by the Prophet (*Adab al-Ma'ishah wa-Akhlaq al-Nubuwah*), translated by L. Zolondek and published also by Brill; and Book II of the first quarter, *i.e., the Kitab Qawa'id al-'Aqa'id* (The Foundations of the Articles of Faith), translated by the present writer and published also by M. Ashraf.

The following pages present in English garb Book III of the first quarter, namely, *the Kitab Asrar al-Taharah* (On the Mysteries of Purity). Though not one of the more profound contributions of al-Ghazzali, it still remains an integral part of the *Ihya'* and should not, therefore, be neglected. The translation is based on three printed texts and one in manuscript form. The printed texts are : first, that Printed at Kafr al-Zaghari in A.H. 1352 from the older Cairo edition of A.H. 1289 ; second, that contained in the text of the *Ithaf al-Sadah al-Muttaqin bi-Sharh Ihya' 'Ulum al-Din* of al-Sayyid al-Murtada al-Zabidi (d.1791) ; third, that reproduced in the margin of the same *Ithaf al-Sadah*; and fourth, the text preserved in a four volume manuscript in the Garrett Collection of Arabic Manuscripts in the Princeton University Library (No.1481). In the translation of Quranic verses, I have depended mainly on J. M. Rodwell's version.

It is my hope that by making still another Book of the *Ihya'* available in English, non-Arabic-speaking scholars will draw a benefit, even from my mistakes.

Nabih Amin Faris

Beirut,
March 29, 1966

CONTENTS

Preface iv
Introduction 1

On Purification from Impurities
That which is Removed 12
The Vehicle of Removal 14
The Manner of Removal 21

Purification from Excrements
The Etiquette of Answering the Call of Nature 23
The Manner of Ablution 29
The Excellence of Ablution 38
The Manner of the Major Ablution 40
The Manner of Purification with Sand 42

On Cleanliness and Cleansing
Discharges 45
Bodily Growths 58

BOOK III

On the Mysteries of Purity which is the Third Book in the Quarter on the Acts of Worship.

In the name of God the Merciful, the Compassionate.

Praise be to God Who has shown kindness unto His servants and thus endued them with cleanliness; who for the purification of their inward thoughts has made His light and grace to flow into their hearts; and for the washing of their bodies has given them water smooth and soft. And may the peace of God be upon the Prophet Muhammad, who has encompassed the entire world from one end to another with the light of guidance, as well as upon his noble and righteous family—a peace the blessing of which will be a salavation unto us or the day of resurrection, and a bulwark unto us against every danger or affliction.

The Prophet said, "Religion was founded on cleanliness."[1] And again, "Purification is the key to

1. Unidentified.

prayer.[2] God said, "Therein are men who aspire to purity, and God loveth the purified."[3] The Prophet also said, "Purification is one half of belief.[4] God also said, "God desireth not to lay a burden upon you, but He desireth to purify you."[5] Through these externals, those who possess insight a woke to the fact that the most important thing is the purification of the heart, because , it is very unlikely that the words of the Propeht, "Purification is one half of belief" meant that men should polish and clean the body with a generous use of water and to neglect the heart and leave it stuffed with impurities and filth.

Purity has four stages: The first stage is the purification of the body from excrements, impurities, and bodily growths and discharges[6]. The second stage is the purification of the bodily senses from crimes and sins. The third stage is the purification of the heart from blameworthy traits and reprehensible vices. The fourth stage is the purification of the inmost self (*sirr*) from everything except God. This last stage is that of the Prophets and saints.

---

2. Ahmad ibn-Hanbal, Taharah: 181; al-Darimi, Tahara; 21; al-Tirmidhi, Taharah:3.

3. Surah IX: 109.

4. Muslim, Taharah: 1; al-Darimi, Taharah:2.

5. Surah v:9.

6. Ar. *fadalat*, sing. *fadlah*, a term used for all bodily growths and discharges which are usually removed by such operations as manciuring, shaving the head and beard, and circumcision.

In everyone of these stages purity is half the activities it entails. For the supreme aim of the activities of the inmost self is to have the majesty and greatness of God revealed unto it. But the knowledge of God will never actually descend into the inmost self unless everything other than God is removed therefrom. For this reason God said, "Say: It is God: then leave them in their pastime of cavilling*." It is evident therefore that [the knowledge of God and allegiance to another besides Him] cannot inhabit the same heart and God has not created for man two hearts within him.

As to the activities of the heart, their supreme purpose is to adorn it [113] with the praiseworthy traits and the doctrines established by the Law. No one who has not cleansed his heart from their opposite, namely the false doctrines and the reprehensible vices, has ever been described by these traits. Hence the purification of the heart comprises one half of its activities. This first half is a prerequisite for the second. It is in this manner that purification is one half of belief. Similarly the purification of the bodily senses from the forbidden things is one half of the activities they entail and is the prerequisite of the second half. Their purification is the first half and their adornment with good works is the second half. These then are the different stages of belief and every stage has its own rank. No one will attain the higher stage unless he goes first through the lower one. He will not reach the purification of the inmost self from the

* *surah* iv:91.

blameworthy qualities and will not adorn it with those which are praiseworthy unless he accomplishes first the purification of the heart from the blameworthy traits and adorns it with the praiseworthy. Similarly no one will attain the purification of the heart from the blameworthy traits or adorn it with the praiseworthy unless he accomplishes first the purification of the bodily senses from the forbidden things and adorns them with good works. The more precious and noble the desired object becomes the more difficult is the way of its attainment, the longer is the road which leads to it, and the greater are the obstacles which block its path. Do not think, therefore, that this can be attained through mere wishing or achieved through no effort. For he whose insight fails to distinguish between these different stages will not perceive of them except the lowest which is equivalent to the last and outermost husk of the desired fruit. He will therefore concentrate upon it and will go to the extreme in the study of its rules, wasting all his time in abstersion (*istinja'*)**, washing clothes, cleaning his body, and outdoing himself in the use of running water, thinking, as a result of a constant fear with which he is obsessed and of a hallucination which dwells in his mind, that the desired and noble purity comprises only such outward and external cleanliness, and revealing thereby a complete ignorance of the life of the early Muslims: how they expended all their energy and thought on the purification of the heart and were very lenient concerning the body, to the extent that 'Umar,

---

** See al-Darimi, Salah; 10-13; ibn-Majah. Taharah:15-16.

despite his high station, has once performed his ablution with water from a jar which belonged to a Christian woman.[7] [In the same spirit] it was customary for the early Muslims not to wash their hands from the remains of fat and food but instead wipe their fingers off against the arches of their feet, regarding the use of alkali (*ushnan*) an innovation. They used to pray, kneeling and prostrating themselves directly on the ground, and walk the streets barefooted. Those who placed nothing between themselves and the earth when they slept were of the greatest among them. They confined themselves exclusively to the use of stone for abstersion.

Abu-Hurayrah and others besides him of the refugees of the mosque-vestibule (*ahlal-Suffah*) said, "We were wont to eat the roasted meat and, wiping our fingers against the pebbles and rubbing them with earth, proceed to prayer repeating the magnificat (*takbir*).[8] Said 'Umar, "We had no knowledge of alkali at the time of the Apostle of God, and our towels were the hollows of our feet: whenever we ate anything we wiped our hands against our feet."[9]

It is said that the first innovations to appear after the death of the Apostle of God were four, namely the use of sieves [for flour], the use of alkali

7. *Cf.* al-Bukhari, Wudu:44.

8. *Cf.* ibn-Majah, At'imah: 29.

9. Ib, 15.

[for washing], the use of tables [for eating], and eating to satiety.

Thus the only concern of the early Muslims was the cleanliness of the heart. One of them even said, "To perform prayer with the shoes on is better than performing it without them because when the Apostle of God took his shoes off during prayer, as Gabriel informed him that they were unclean, and the people present took their shoes off as well, he told them, 'Why have you taken off your shoes?'"][10]

Concerning those who take their shoes off for prayer al-Nakha'i[11] said disapproving the practice, "I wish that someone in need would pass by and take these shoes away [never to return them]."

Such then was their lenience on these affairs. In fact they used to walk barefooted in muddy streets, sit on the mud, and kneel and prostrate themselves in prayer directly on the floors of the mosques. They were wont to eat bread made of wheat and barley, both of which were trodden by the feet of animals and polluted with their urine. They made no effort to avoid the sweat of camels and horses despite the fact that both animals were constantly wallowing in impure things. Not a single question concerning the niceties of impurities has come down to us from them. Such then was their lenience in these matters. But the situation has now come to such a

10. For a tradition of the same import, of, abu Dawud, Taharah:137.

11. Ibrahim ibn-Yazid, A II 96-A.D. 714-5. See ibn Qutaybah p.235; Tahdhib al-Asma, pp.135-36.

pass where a certain group of people who consider their makeup (*ru'unah*) equivalent to cleanliness and say that it is the foundation of religion. They spend the greater part of their time in beautifying their bodies, just as the hairdresser does with the bride, but neglect their hearts and leave them desolate, stuffed with the foul impurities of pride, conceit, ignorance, hypocrisy, and deceit; and neither disapprove of them nor show any amazement at them. Furthermore, if any one should confine himself to the use of stones for abstersion, or walk barefooted on the ground, or pray on the floor or on the bare mats of the mosque without spreading a rug over either, or walk over the rugs [of the mosque] without leather overshoes, or perform his ablution with water from a jar belonging to an old woman or an irreligious man, they would clamour and raise a vociferous outcry over him, call him filthy, ostracise him from their midst, and disdain from eating with him or associating with him. On the other hand they regard austerity in attire, which is a part of belief,[12] filth; [114] while make-up and ornamentation they consider cleanliness. See then how the evil has become good, and the good evil; how the form of religion has disappeared just as its truth and knowledge have disappeared.

If you will ask, "Will you then say that those practices which the Sufis have started in connexion with their outward appearance and matters of cleanliness are forbidden and evil?" I shall say, "Far

12. *Cf.* Ibn-Majah, Zuhd:4.

be it from me to generalize on this subject and not treat every case on its own merit." Nevertheless this shall I say, "This excessive cleaning and these painful undertakings, the preparation of special vessels and paraphernalia, the use of overshoes, wearing veils for protection against the dust and other similar devices, if they were examined by themselves without reference to anything else, they will be found permissible. Certain situations and motives may become attached to them and will render them at one time good and at another evil. That in themselves they are permissible is quite evident since he who practises them does so on his own account in his own body and clothes. He, therefore, may do whatever he wishes so long as there is neither waste nor extravagance therein. They become evil when they are made a fundamental part of religion and are consequently advanced as the interpretation of the words of the Prophet. "Religion was founded on cleanliness." As a result those who are not very strict in the observance of all these rules of cleanliness but, like the early Muslims, are lenient therein, are subjected to harsh strictures. Again they become evil when they are performed for the purpose of adorning the body and beautifying it. This, in fact, is hypocrisy, which is forbidden. By these two considerations will they become evil.

They are good practices when their purpose is utility rather than ornamentation; when he who fails to observe them is not censured; when prayer is not delayed on their account; and when they do not prevent the individual from doing something better or hinder him from pursuing a superior knowledge and the like. When none of these things is attached to them they are permissible and may even be considered meritorious through the good motive behind them. But these practices are possible only to the idle, who if they do not spend their time in them will waste it in sleep or useless conversation. Consequently to spend this [otherwise wasted] time of theirs in these practices becomes the more worthy, because any time spent in purification renews the remembrance of God and that of the acts of worship. There is, therefore, no harm in them provided they do not become evil or extravagant.

As to the men of learning and action, they should not spend any of their time in these practices except what is necessary. For to go to excess is evil just as to waste one's life, which is the best and most precious pearl, when it should be preserved and utilized, is evil. None need wonder at that since the good works of the righteous are the evil works of the favourites of God. The idle should not neglect cleanliness himself and disapprove of it in the Sufis claiming that he is thereby emulating the Companions. For to emulate the Companions truly is not to devote oneself except to that which is more important than external cleanliness. Thus it was said to Dawud al-Tai[13] "Why do you not comb you beard?" He replied, "Do you think I have nothing else to do?" For this reason I do not think that the

---

13. Dawud ibn-Nusayr al-Ta'i A.H. 165 A.D. 781-82. See ibn-Sa'd, Vol. VI, p.255; ibn Qutaybah, p.257.

learned man or the student, or the labourer should waste their time washing their clothes in order to avoid wearing the clothes which the laundry-man has washed because they imagine that the latter has not cleaned the clothes well enough. As a matter of fact the early Muslims used to perform their prayers while wearing tanned fur-coats, and none of them was known to differentiate between laundered clothes and tanned fur-coats as far as purity and impurity were concerned. Rather they avoided all impurities wherever and whenever they saw them and paid no attention to remote and subtle possibilities. They, however, scrutinized very carefully the subtleties of hypocrisy and injustice, so that Sufyan al-Thawri once told a companion who raised his eyes to see an elaborate and exquisite doorway by which they had just passed, "Do not do that! For if people would not look at this door its owner would not have been so extravagant. Verily those who look at his door help him to be extravagant." Thus [the early Muslims] spent all the efforts of their minds in pointing out such subtleties rather than in speculating on the remote possibilities of impurity.

Therefore it will be better for the learned man to find for himself an ordinary person to wash his clothes carefully for him, because, from the point of view of lenience, this is better. The ordinary person will benefit by his work since he will then give his soul which urges to evil something permissible to kepp it busy and consequently keep it from sinning. For the soul, unless it is kept busy with something, will lead to trouble. Furthermore, if the ordinary man wishes to gain the favour of the learned man through this work, he will find it to be one of the best means to gain his end. Again, the time of the learned man is too precious to be one of the best means to gain his end. Again, the time of the ordinary man is spent in such work, and he will benefit in every respect.

Let this illustration, therefore, serve men as a reminder of other similar works and activities, to determine their different values and to establish their order of preference. For care in preserving the hours of life and expending them in pursuing the best is more important than being particular and fastidious concerning the minute affairs of this world.

Having acquainted yourself with this introduction and found out that purity has four stages, then know that in this book we shall not discuss anything except the fourth stage which is the cleanliness of the body, because, in the first half of the book we purposely do not address ourselves except to external and outward things.

We, therefore, say that the purification of the body is divided into three parts: purification from impurities, purification from excrements, and purification from bodily growths and discharges, which is accomplished by such operations as manicuring, shaving, removing the hair off the pubes with a depilatory, circumcision, and the like.

PART I

On Purification from Impurities, the Examination of which Involves a Study of that which is Removed, the Vehicle of Removal, and the Manner of Removal.

THAT WHICH IS REMOVED

That which is removed (*al-muzal*) [115] is impurity. Substances (*a'yan*) are of three kinds: inanimate objects, animate objects and parts of animate objects.

As to inanimate objects, all, except wine and intoxication beverages, are pure. As to animate objects, all, except the dog and the pig and their products, are pure. When animate objects die, they are all impure except five, namely human beings, fish, locusts, apple worms, and, of the same category as apple worms, is every food which changes, as well as every form of life which has no flowing blood like flies beetles, and the like. Water is not rendered impure when such objects fall into it.

As to the parts of inanimate objects, they are of two kinds. The first comprises those things which may be cut off and its rule is the same as that of dead bodies. [One exception is] the hair which is not rendered impure by shearing and death. Bones, however, are rendered impure by death. The second comprises all wet things which the body exudes or emits. Everything which is not subject to change and has no fixed seat like tears and sweat are pure. But saliva and the mucus of the nose, and whatever things which have a fixed seat and are subject to change, are all impure except the seed of life like semen and eggs. Pus, blood, feces, and urine are impure in all animals. Nothing is exempted of these impurities except five things. The first, the remains of ordure after abstersion with stones— whatever does not extend beyond the orifice is exempted. Second, the mud in the streets and the dust of [dried up] dung, despite the fact that their impurity is established, are exempt only to the extent to which they cannot be avoided, i.e., which is not the result of negligence or oversight. Third, what hangs to the bottom of the shoes of impurities, of which the streets are always full. This is exempt, after it has been wiped off, because of necessity. Fourth, the blood of fleas—little or much—except when it goes beyond the ordinary limits—whether it be on your own shirt or in some one else's shirt, which you may wear. Fifth, the blood of pimples and the pus they discharge. Ibn-'Umar once wiped off a pimple on his face and it bled but he went ahead and performed his prayer without first washing. Of the same category is what chronic boils discharge as well as the blood which issues after phlebotomy, except in such cases where the issue of blood is caused by an abcess where it will be subject to the same rule which governs the blood of menstruction and not that of pimples of which man is never always free. The toleration of these five impurities by the Law shows that the principle of purity is lenience and all that was innovated therein is the result of obsessions which have no foundation.

THE VEHICLE OF REMOVAL

The vehicle of removal *(al-muzal bihi)* is either solid or liquid. The solid is the stone of abstersion which has been purified through being [sun-] dried. It should be a hard, pure, and dry stone but not a relic of any veneration.

As to liquids, none of them removes impurities except water and not any kind of water at that, but only the pure water which has not become contaminated through its contact with other bodies. Again water ceases to be pure when, through contact with impurities, it changes in taste or colour or odour. If, on the other hand it does not change in any of these, and its quantity approaches two hundred and fifty manehs, which equals five hundred 'Iraqi rotls, it will not become impure, because the Prophet said, "When water is sufficient to fill two pitchers it carries no impurities."[14] According to al-Shafi'i if it were less, it would become impure. This relates to stagnant water only. Running water, on the other hand, when polluted with impurities, the ripples which have been contaminated with these impurities become impure, except those beneath and below; because the ripples of water are separated one from the other. Similarly, the impurities, if they should flow in the watercourse, render impure the part in which they fall as well as the part to the right and left of the

---

14. *Cf.* al-Tirmidhi, Taharah; 50; abu Dawud, Taharah:33.

part wherein they fall, if the amount of water does not exceed two pitchers. If the flow of the water were faster than the flow of the impurities, what lies over the impurities is pure and what lies below them is impure, no matter how far it may move or how much it may be, unless it gathers in a pond or cavity the size of which is larger than two pitchers. If an amount of impure water, equal to two pitchers, should gather in one place, that water would become pure if mixed [with a larger quantity of pure water]. This is the position of al Shafi'i. I had hoped, however, that his position would be like that of Malik who held that water, no matter how meagre its amount might become, would not be rendered impure except through change [in taste, colour, or odour], because the need for it is great and to lay down the condition of two pitchers would simply provoke suspicion and fear. It has therefore become very difficult to observe this rule and, upon my life, it is difficult; those who would try and examine it would find that out for themselves.

Furthermore, I have no doubt that if such a condition had been stipulated, then Makkah and al-Madinah, because of the scarcity of running water and still water in big quantities in either town, would have been the two most difficult places for achieving purity. Yet from the time of the Apostle of God to the last days of his Companions not a single crisis pertaining to purification nor a single question concerning the manner of safeguarding water from impurities had been reported. The vessles in which their water was placed was handled by boys and slave-girls who were not careful against impurities:

Furthermore, 'Umar performed his ablution with water from the jar of a Christian woman. This act of 'Umar is just as clear and binding as a genuine tradition which fulfils all requirements (*sarih*) in establishing that water becomes impure only when it changes [in taste, or colour, or odour]. Otherwise the impurity of the Christian woman and that of her vessels are quite evident and are very readily discerned. Therefore this position becomes uptenable. The fact that no question concerning it arose during the days of the Apostle and his Companions is one proof for its being untenable; the action of 'Umar is another; while a third proof is found in the fact that the Apostle of God was wont to incline [116] the water vessel to the cat and to leave all vessels unprotected against it even after he had seen it eat a mouse.[15] Nowhere in their land were tanks set apart for cats to drink. Nor did the cats go down to the bottom of the well for water.

The fourth proof is that al-Shafi'i has definitely said that water with which a certain impurity has been washed was pure, as long as it did not undergo any change [in taste, or colour, or odour], and was impure whenever it did undergo any such change. And what difference is there between water contaminated with impurities through its own contact with them or through the contact of impurities with it? And what sense is there in saying that the force of the contact of water prevents impurity although contact in itself does not hinder the intermixture of impurity? If the one

15. Al-Tirmidhi, Taharah, 69; ibn-Majah, Taharah;32.

is to be explained on the grounds of need and necessity, need and necessity are also present in the other. There is no difference between pouring water into a vessel wherein there is an impure garment and throwing the impure garment in a vessel wherein there is pure water-both being ordinary practices in laundry and washing.

A fifth proof is found in the fact that it was the practice to perform abstersion along the edges of small bodies of running water. There is no disagreement concerning the position of al-Shafi'i that if urine should fall into running water and the water does not undergo any change [in taste, or colour or odour], it will still remain permissible to use the water for ablution no matter how small the quantity. And what difference is there between running and still water. Upon my life, which is the stronger argument: to base the decision on the lack of change in the water or on the force of its flow? Furthermore, what are the limitations of this force? Does it extend to the water which flows within the pipes of baths or not? If it does not extend to the water which flows within the pipes of baths, what accounts for the difference? And if it does extend to such water that is the difference between what falls into it and what falls into its course as it is poured out from vessels over the body, when both are running waters? Furthermore, if it is to be ruled that water which flows over a solid and stationary impurity is impure, although it does not undergo any change, and that it remains impure until a quantity equal to two pitchers collects in a small pond, [it should be remembered] that urine is intermixed with running water more readily than any solid and stationary object possibly could. And what difference is there between the solid and liquid [impurities] when the water is the same and admixture is more through-going than mere contact?

The sixth proof is found in the fact that if a rotl of urine was poured into a quantity of water equal to two pitchers and then the water was distributed into different vessels. Water drawn from any of these vessels is pure; yet it is wellknown that urine, though a small quantity of it, contaminates all. Which is more convincing to explain; that the water is pure because it underwent no change, or because of its large quantity, even after that quantity has ceased to be large, and despite the knowledge that a part of the impurity still exists in the reminder of that water?

A seventh proof is seen in the fact that in bygone days ascetics constantly performed their ablutions in public baths and dipped their hands and vessels in tanks despite the small quantity of water these tanks contained and despite their knowledge that both pure and impure hands have been dippped into these tanks.

These incidents together with urgent need and necessity strengthen the belief that only the lack of any change in the water was taken into consideration whenever its purity was questioned, relying thereby on the words of the Apostle when he said, "Water was created pure and nothing renders it impure except that which changes its taste, or colour or odour.'[16] There is a basic truth in this, namely that it is the property of every liquid to transform whatever may fall into it into its own, provided that liquid be the dominant element of the two. Thus just as the dog when it falls into a mine of salt, is itself transformed into salt, and through its transformation into salt and its loss of caninity, becomes pure, so is the case with vinegar and milk, whenever they are placed in water which is dominant, they lose their properties and acquire those of the water, unless the vinegar and the milk be the dominant elements, in which case they will prevail. Their prevalence is known through the presence of their taste, or colour, or odour. This then is the criterion [whereby things are determined and judged]. To it the Law has pointed in the case of the water which is capable of removing impurities. It is, therefore, worthy of being relied upon. Consequently, through it the guilt is lifted [off those who use water which the fastidious deem impure], and the meaning [of the tradition that water was created pure] is explained through it since water prevails over impurities and renders the objects pure, just as it was shown in the case of the two pitchers, as well as in the case of the used water, and the running water, and in the case of inclining the vessel for the cat.

Do not, however, think that that is an exemption, for it were so it would have been like the remains of ordure after abstersion and the blood of fleas: it would be deemed pure until [through

16. *Cf.* ibn-Majah, Taharah:76.

excess] it makes the water impure. Even when the quantity is small, water is not rendered impure by articles steeped or washed therein or by a cat licking therefrom.

As to the saying of the Apostle that water carries no impurities, it is in itself ambiguous, for whenever water undergoes change it carries impurities. If it be said that the Apostle meant with his words that water carries no impurities so long as it undergoes no change, it will then be possible to say that in most cases water does not undergo any change through its contact with ordinary impurities. Furthermore, the words of the tradition imply the acceptance that when the quantity of water is short of two pitchers, the water carries impurities when brought into contact with them. Nevertheless, it is quite possible to ignore the implied meaning of the tradition for lesser reasons than those we have already mentioned in those seven proofs. The apparent meaning of the words of the Apostle that water carries no impurities is to negate the act of carrying—in other words it transform impurities to its own property, just as we say that a mine of salt will not hold a dog or anyting else but will decompose and transform them into salt. Men perform their abstersion in small waters and streamlets and dip impure vessels therein, and then wonder whether or not the water has undergone any perceptible change. It has therefore become evident that whenever the quantity of waters exceeds two pitchers, ordinary impurities do not cause it to undergo any change.

If you should say that the Prophet had said that water carries no impurities, no matter how much these impurities increase, then the argument would be turned against you, because whenever the impurities increase in quantity, water would carry them in effect as well as in fact. For this reason, I would say that it is imperative for both schools[17] to be specific and limit their interpretation to the ordinary impurities.

In short, in the case of ordinary impurities, I am inclined to be tolerant and lenient, following therein the example of the early Muslims and hoping thereby to do away with fears and suspicions. In that spirit have I given my legal opinions concerning disputed problems of purity.

THE MANNER OF REMOVAL

[117] If an impurity is an impurity in effect (*hukmiyah*), *i.e.,* it has no palpable body, it is sufficient to run water over all its parts. But if it is an impurity in fact, *i.e.,* physical (*'ayniyah*) it is necessary to remove the physical. The persistence of the taste indicates the persistence of the physical. The same is true of the persistence of colour except in such cases where the impurity leaves an indeliable stain, in which event it is exempted, provided it has been thoroughly rubbed and washed. But the persistence of odour indicates the persistence of the physical and in not exempted except in such cases where the object has a strong odour which is difficult to remove, in which event

17. The Malikite and the Sahfi'ite.

soaking it in water and wringing it several successive times will do instead of rubbing and washing as in the case of the persistence of colour. It will do away with fear and suspicion to know that things have been created pure. Objects on which impurities are not positively seen may be used in prayer, and one should not resort to deduction to prove the presence of impurities.

PART II

Purification from Excrements

The purification from excrements (*ahdath*) comprises ablutions (*wudu*), major ablution (*ghusl*), and purification with sand (*tayammum*), and are preceded by abstersion (*istinja*). We shall now state the manner of their performance in the prescribed order together with their etiquette and rules, beginning with the reason for ablution and the etiquette of answering the call of nature.

THE ETIQUETTE OF ANSWERING THE CALL OF NATURE

[The person] should go into the wilderness far from the eyes of onlookers.[18] HE should shelter himself behind something whenever possible and should not unconver his nakedness (*'awrah*) before he reaches the place of squatting. He should not face the sun or the moon with his nakedness, nor should he face the qiblah or turn his back unto it when his nakedness is uncovered except when he is within a house, and even then it is better to avoid [that position].[19] It is permissible for him, when in

18. *Cf.* ibn-Majah, Taharah;22.

19. Ibn-Majah, Taharah: 17, 18; al-Tirmidhi, Taharah:51.

the wilderness, to shelter himself behind his camel or use for that purpose his skirt. He should avoid squatting down [for the purpose of answering the call of nature] in any place where it is customary for men to meet for conversation. He should not urinate in still water,[20] or under a fruite tree, or in any enclosure.[21] When urinating he should keep away from hard surface and windy places in order to avoid spatter and splash. When he squats down to answer the call of nature, he should support himself on the left leg. When entering a house to urinate he should advance with the left leg first and when he leaves he should advance with the right. Furthermore, he should not urinate while standing. 'A'ishah said, "He who tells that the Prophet was wont to urinate standing, believe him not.[22] 'Umar also said, "The Apostle of God once saw me urinate while standing and he told me, 'O 'Umar! Do not urinate standing,' Henceforth, never urinated standing."[23] Yet in certain instances, it is allowed since Hudhayafah related that the Apostle once urinated standing and that Hudayfah then brought him water for ablution which he performed and wiped his shoes off.[24]

---

20. Ibn-Majah, Taharah: 25, al-Tirmidhi, Taharah:6.

21. Abu-Dawud, Taharah:16.

22. Al-Tirmidhi, Taharah;8.

23. *Ibid*, Taharah:8.

24. Tavalisi. 406: abu-Dawud Taharah: 12, *cf*, al-Tirmidhi, Taharah: 9; ibn-Majah, Taharah:8.

Again no one should urinate in the bath tub. In this connexion the Prophet said that most of men's fears and suspicions whether or not things are pure result from urinating in bath tubs.[25] Ibn-al-Mubarak said, "However, if the water in the bath tub be running water, then there is no harm in urinating therein."

When a person proceeds to answer the call of nature, he should not take with him anything which contains the name of God or of His Apostle.[26] He should not enter the water-closet bareheaded, and on entering he should say, "I seek refuge in God against the accursed Satan, the filthy, the impure, the abominable, the pernicious"[27] On leaving the water-closet he should say, "praise be to God Who hath removed from me that which is harmful and hath left me that which is useful."[28] He should say this after he had left the water-closet. He should prepare the stones [for abstersion] before squatting, and should not perform the act of abstersion over the place where he had defecated. He should take the utmost pains in cleaning his penis from urine by shaking it to and from three times and by stroking its lower extremity with his hand.[29] Nevertheless, he should not worry too much over

---

25. Abu-Dawud, Taharah: 15; ibn-Majah, Taharah:12.

26. *Cf* abu-Dawud Taharah: 14; ibn-Majah, Taharah.11.

27. *Cf* Ibn-Majah, Taharah: 9; al-Tirmidhi, Taharah: 4; al-Bukhari, Wudu:9.

28. *cf.* al-Tirmidhi, Taharah: 5; ibn-Majah, Taharah:10.

29. *Cf.* Ibn-Majah, Taharah:19.

the state of his cleanliness lest he become victim to an obsession which will wear him out. If he should feel something wet there, let him suppose that it is nothing but some of the water [with which he performed the act of abstersion]. If this does not allay his suspicion let him sprinkle some water on the place so that he can then assure himself that the wetness is caused by water not by urine. Consequently, he will not allow Satan to prevail over him through fear and suspicion. The Propeht himself, we are told in a tradition, has done the same thing, namely, sprinkled water over [his orifice][30]. The person who was wont to exert the least effort in affecting the cleanliness of his orifice was the most learned among them, for fear and obsessions indicate lack of learning and ignorance.

In a tradition Salman [al-Farisi] said, "The Apostle of God taught us [118] everything, even how to answer the call of nature: Hew commanded us not to perform the act of abstersion with either bone or [dried] dung, and forbade us to face the qiblah when defecating or urinating."[31]

A certain Bedouin having fought with one of the Companions told him, "You do not even know how to defecate." The Companion answered and said, " Yea, by your father's beards, I do, and I am a past master at it. I go out far into the wilderness, prepare the stones [for abstersion], face the wormwood, turn my back to the wind, squat like the

---

30. *Ibid*,;58.

31. Ibn Majah, Taharah:16.

deer, and stoop raising my posterior as the ostrich raises its tail," (The wormwood is an aromatic desert plant, squatting is crouch-resting on his toes, and stooping is raising the posterior part).

It is sometimes allowed for the man to urinate close to his companion provided he be concealed and sheltered. The Apostle of God has done that despite his extreme shyness, in order to show men that it was permissible.[32]

The Manner of Abseteršion

The person will then perform the abstersion for his posterior orifice with three stones. If the orifice is cleansed therewith, the three stones will suffice, otherwise, a fourth stone must be used, and if this proves sufficient, a fifth must be used, because [although] only cleanliness is necessary, the use of an odd number [of stones] is desirable. The Prophet said, "When thou employest stones for thy abstersion, use an odd number."[33] In performing the abstersion, the person should hold the stone with his left hand, place it at the fore-part of his orifice just before the seat of impurity, and run it over with horizontal and circular motion to the rear part. He should then take the second stone, place it at the rear part and run it over to the forepart. Taking then the third stone he should run it around the orifice. If he should not be able to run the stone around the orifice, he might perform the act in parts.

---

32. *Cf.* al-Bukhari, Wudu' : 64.

33. Al-Bukhari, Wudu':25, 26, Ibn Majah, Taharah 23, 44.

He then should take a large stone with his right and his penis with the left and with it(the left) move the penis thereby wiping it against the stone in there different places, or against three stones, or against three different palces on a wall, until he sees wetness on the place where he had wiped his penis. If that is accomplished after he wiped it twice, he should do it a third time. This is obligatory if he wishes to limit himself to the use of stones. If that is accomplished after he had wiped his penis four times against the stone, it would be desirable to wipe it a fifth time for the sake of maintaining an odd number.

He should then move to another place and perform the act of abstersion with water, pouring it over the seat of excrement and rubbing it with the left until nothing which the palm of the hand could feel is left. He should not go to excess by trying to remove the parts which are still within the orifice because such a thing would give rise to obsession. He should realise that whatever water cannot reach lies within, and these parts which lie within are not subject to the rule that governs impurities unless they come out. And everything which is external and which is subject to the rule that governs impurities fulfils the difinition of purity when the water reaches and removes it. There is, therefore, no sense in being victim to an obsession in this repsect.

At the end of abstersion the person should say, "O my God! Purify my heart from hypocrisy, and make my body chaste." He then should wipe his hand against a wall or earth for removing any odour which might have persisted thereon. The use of both stones and water together is desirable, as it was related that when God revealed unto the Apostle the verse, "Therein are men who aspire to purity, and God loveth the purified,"[34] the Apostle said to the people of Quba,[35] "What is the purity for which God has herewith praised you?" They said, "We were wont to use both stones and water [for performing the act of abstersion]."

The Manner of Ablution

When [the person] is through with abstersion, he should proceed to perform his ablution, for never has the Apostle of God been seen emerging after he had answered the call of nature without immediately performing the ablution. The person should commence with the use of the toothpick. Thus the Apostle said, "Your mouths are the pathways of the Qur'an. Render them, therefore clean with toothpicks."[36] His purpose, when using the toothpick, should be the purification of his mouth for the reading of the Qur'an, and the invocation of God in prayer. The Prophet said, "One prayer after the use of the toothpick is better than seventy and five prayers without the use of the

---

34. Surah ix:109.

35. A village, two miles south of al-Madinah, where Muhammad spent for days on his *hijrah* to al-Madinah. He prayed in its mosque, alleged to have been built by his Companions who preceded him to his new capital. See Yaqut, *Buldan*, Vol.IV pp.2-24.

36. Ibn-Majah, Tahara:7.

toothpick."[37] And again,"Had it not been for my fear to overburden my people, I would have commanded them to use the toothpick before every parayer,[38]" And again [119] "Why do you come before me with yellow teeth? Use toothpicks."[39] He also was wont to use the toothpick several times every night. It was also related that ibn-Abbas once said, "The Apostle has so repeatedly commanded us to use the toothpick that we expected him soon to receive a revelation on its use."[40] The Apostle also said, "Use ye the toothpick: it is a purifier for the mouth and well-pleasing unto God."[41] 'Ali said, "The toothpick develops and strengthens the memory and banishes sluggishness." Furthermore, it was customary for the Companions of the Prophet to go about with their toothpicks carried behind the ears.[42]

The manner of its use. For a toothpick men should use the *arak* (salvadora perisce) wood or other rough branches which remove the yellow deposits around the teeth. The toothpick should be used both horizontally and vertically, and if one should limit himself to one of the two motions, let him use it horizontally.

---

37. *Cf.* Ahmad ibn-Hanbal, Tahara: 169.

38. Ahmad ibn-Hanbal, Tahrarh:167, 170.

39. *Ibid.*, Taharah; 165.

40. *Ibid.*, Taharah; 159, 160.

41. *Ibid.*, Taharah: 156, 157, 158.

42. *Cf.* abu-Dawud, Taharah: 25; Ahmad ibn-Hanbal, Taharah:167.

It is desirabel to use the toothpick prior to every prayer· and prior to every ablution whether it is followed with prayer or not. Equally desirable is its use when the taste of the mouth has become bad as a result of sleep, or long abstinence from food, or eating a thing of unpleasant smell.

After completing the cleansing of his mouth with the toothpick the person should then proceed with his ablution facing therein the qiblah, and saying, "In the name of God the Merciful, the Compassionate." The Prophet said, "There is no ablution to him who does not call upon the name of God,"[43] i.e., no complete ablution. The person should then say, "[O God!] I seek refuge in thee from the power of the devil. I seek refuge in thee O God lest they should come and surround me." He then should wash his hands three times before putting them into the vessel and should say, "O God, I ask thee for luck and blessing, and seek refuge in thee against ill-luck and destruction." His purpose should be the removal of excrements or making prayer lawful. He should bear that purpose in mind until he had washed his face. If, however, he happens to forget the purpose of his ablution just before he washes his face, he will not be penalized for it. He then should take up a handful of water with his right, and rinse his mouth with it thrice and gargle, allowing the water to reach his throat, except when he is fasting, at which time he should take it easy [lest he swallow any of it].

---

43. *Cf.* ibn-Majah, Taharah, 41.

Having done that he should say, "O God, Help me to recite Thy book and to glorify Thy name." Thereupon he should take up another handful and inhale it thrice, forcing it with his breath up his nose and flushing thereby its cartilages, and then force the water out by exhaling. As he sniffs the water he should say, "O God! Grant me [to enjoy] the perfumes of Paradise and be gracious unto me." As he exhales in order to force the water out of his nose he should say, "O God! I seek refuge in Thee against the stench of Hell and evil of the world." This is said because inhaling constitutes drawing in and exhaling is removal and rejection.

He then should take another handful of water for his face and should wash it from the beginning of the flat part of the forehead to the extremity of the fore-part of the chin lengthwise, and from ear to ear laterally. The two temples which are on either side of the forehead are not included in the face but form a part of the head. The water is allowed to reach the edge of the bangs which women are wont to affect: It is that part which lies at the side of the face when the end of a thread is placed upon the top of the ear, and the other end is placed upon the corner of the forehead. The water, however, is allowed to reach the four parts of face where the hair grows, namely, the eyebrows, the mustache, the side whiskers, and the eyelashes which are, for the most part sparse. The side whiskers are that part of the beard which grows parellel to and alongside the ears. Water should also be allowed to reach the base of sparse but not thick beards, *i.e.* the frontal part of the face. The rule which governs the hair between the lower lip and the chin is the same as that which governs the beard, whether thick or sparse. He should [wash his face in this prescribed manner] thrice and then pour water over the long part of his beard, and work his fingers in and clean the eye holes and [the inner corners of the eyes] where the dirt which they discharge collects and [the outer corners] where the kohl gathers, for it was related that the Prophet himself did that.[44] When the person washes his eyes his wish should be that sin would depart therfrom. Similarly at the washing of every member of his body, he should wish for the departure of sin therefrom. As he washes his face, he should say, "O God! Cleanse Thou my face with Thy light when Thou cleanseth the faces of Thy saints; and [120] blacken not my face with Thy darkness when Thou rendereth the faces of Thy enemies black." When washing his face, he should also let water flow in the interstices of his beard, for, it is desirable.

He should then wash his arms up to the elbows three times, [When washing his hands] he should move the ring around his finger. He then should draw his wetten right hand over the fore-part of his head, [raising his head gear with the left], and should apply water to the upper part of the upper arm. For [the believers] will appear on the day of resurrection with whiteness on their foreheads, wrists, and ankles, from the effect of ablution.[45] Similarly, a traditon declares that the Propeht said, "Whoever is able to clean the fore-part of his head

44. Unidentified.

45. Al-Bukhari, Wudu:3.

let him do so."[46] It has also been related that the whiteness[47] appears on those parts of the body which are washed at the time of ablution[48].

The person should begin with the washing of his right hand and say, "O God! [On the day of judgment] hand me the book of my actions in my right hand and judge me with lenience." When he washes his left he should say, "I beseech Thee O God, hand me not the book of my action in my left or from behind my back." He then should proceed to wipe his head thoroughly by soaking his hands in the water, bringing the tips of their fingers, both the right and the left, together, placing them on the forepart of the head, running them over to the opposite side, and finally bringing them back again to the forepart. All this constitutes one wiping. He should go through it thrice and say, "Cover me with Thy mercy, O God, and shower upon me of Thy blessings. Give me to sit in the shadow of Thy throne on that day when there will be no shade except Thine own."

He then should wipe his ears, both outside and inside, with fresh water. To do this, he should put the tips of his forefingers into his ears and twist them round, passing his thumbs at the same time over their back. He then should place the palms of his hands over the outer part of his ears, repeating the act thrice and saying, "Make me O God one of

46. *Ibid.*

47. Ar. *Hilyah*, which means literally ornament.

48. Muslims, Taharah:40.

those who hear and pattern their work in accordance to the best of what they hear. O God, let me hear the crier of Paradise with the righteous."

He should then wipe his neck with fresh water, because the Apostle said, "Wiping the neck safeguards against being shackled on the day of resurrection."[49] As he wipes his neck he should say, "O God, release my neck from [the yoke of] fire and save Thou me from the chains and shackles." He should then wash his right foot thrice and, with his left hand, pass his fingers between his toes from the bottom up, beginning with the little toe of the right foot and ending with the little toe of the left. [As he washes his right foot] he should say, "O God, steady my foot on the narrow bridge on that day when feet slip down into the fires of Hell." And as he washes his left foot he should say, "I seek thy aid O God lest my foot should slip off the bridge on that day when the feet of the hypocrites slip." [In washing his feet] he should let the water reach half way up his legs. When he is through, he should turn his head up to heaven and say, "I testify that there is no god but Allah, that He hath no associate, and that Muhammad is His servant and apostle. Glory be to Thee O God, and the praise be Thine, for there is no god but Thee. I have done evil and sinned against my own soul. I beg Thy forgiveness O God, and I hearken back unto Thee. Forgive, therefore, my sin and be gracious unto me; Thou art the Forgiving, the Merciful. Give me to be penitent O God, and make me pure. Grant me to be one of Thy righteous servants and make me patient and grateful. Help me always to remember Thy name, and to praise Thee day and night." It is said that whoever repeats

49. Unidentified.

this [collect] after performing his ablutions will have the seal of approval affixed to his performance and will have a place prepared for him beneath the throne, wherefrom he will continue to praise God and glorify His Holy Name. His reward will be preserved for him until the day of resurrection.

Several things are undesirable during ablution. Of these is to wash [each member] more than thrice. Whoever goes beyond the three transgresses. Another undesirable thing is to be extravagant in the use of water. The Prophet performed his ablution, washing each member thrice, and said, "Whoever goes beyond three transgresses and does evil."[50] And again, "There will rise among this people some who will be extravagant in their supplications and purity"[51] It is also said, "A sure sign of weakness in man's learning is his fondness for water during the act of purification." Ibrahim ibn-Adham said, "Obsessions grow out of [fastidiousness in] purification."

Among the undesirable things also are speaking during ablution and splashing the face with water. Others also objected to the use of towels after ablution saying that the water used in the act is weighed [on the day of resurrection]. This was said by both sa'id ibn-al-Musayyab and al-Zuhri.[52] But Mu'adh related that the Apostle himself wiped his face [after ablution] with the end of his garment.[53] 'A'ishah also related that he had a towel [which he

50. Abu Dawud, Taharah:52.

51. *Ibid*, 45.

52. Probably abu-Salamah ibn-'Abd-al-Rahman. A.H. 94 A.D. 713, Tadhkirat-al-Huffaz, Vol.I, p.59.

53. Al-Tirmidhi, Taharah:20.

used after ablution][54]. The authenticity of this tradition has, however, been questioned.[55]

It is also undesirable to perform the act of ablution from water contained in brass vessles; or to use for that purpose water which has been heated in the sun. This latter thing is undesirable for medical reasons. The objection to the use of water contained in brass vessles was related on the authority of ibn-'Umar and abu-Hurayrah.[56] [121] A certain person said, "I brought out for Shu'bah[57] water in brass vessel but he refused to perform his ablution therefrom." In this objection to brass vessels he followed the example of ibn-'Umar and abu-Hurayrah.

When the person completes his ablution and proceeds to pray he must, no doubt, be aware of his external purity, the purity which men behold and see. He should, however, be ashamed of communing with God without first purifying his heart, which God beholds and sees. He should know with certainty that the purity of the heart is accomplished through repentance, putting aside blameworthy traits, and laying hold on those which are praiseworthy. He who limits himself to external purity and cleanliness is like the person who, desiring to invite a king to his house, embarks on

---

54. *Ibid*, Taharah:40.

55. Al-Tirmidhi himself, in narrating the tradition, casts doubt on its authenticity.

56. *Cf.* Ibn-Majah, Taharah:61, where the same thing is permissible.

57. Abu-Bistam Shu'bah ibn-al-Hajjaj al-'Ataki, A.H. 160-A.D. 776-7; see ibn-Sa'd, Vol. 7, Pt 2 p.38; *Tadhkirat-al-Huffaz*. Vol. I. pp.181-85

the task of plastering and whitewashing its outer gate, but neglects the interior, leaving it stuffed with all manner of dirt and filth. Such a man is best fitted for contempt and perdition. But God knoweth best.

The Excellence of Ablution

The Apostle of God said, "Whoever performs his ablution well and prostrates himself twice in prayer without allowing anything worldly to distract his mind, will be absolved of all his sins, and will become as innocent as he was when he was born.[58] Or according to another version "without permitting his mind to wander, will be forgiven all his past sins."[59]

The Apostle also said: "Let me tell you wherewith God atones sin and raises the ranks [of the faithful]: Performing the ablution though in distress, frequenting the mosques, and looking forward for the time of the next prayer. Verily this is the threefold bond."[60] The Apostle performed the ablution throwing water once on every member and said, "Prayer is unacceptable before God except after such ablution."[61] He performed the ablution throwing water twice and said, "Whoever performs the ablution throwing water twice on every member will twice receive his reward from God."[62] Finally, he performed the ablution throwing water thrice and said, "This is my manner of ablution and that of

58. *Cf.* Ahmad ibn-Hanbal, Taharah: 183, 188.

59. *Cf.* al-Darimi Taharah:43.

60. *Cf.* Ahmad ibn-Hanbal, Taharah-193.

61. *Cf.* Al-Bukhar, Wudu' :22.

62. *Cf. ibid*, Wudu'; 23.

the propehts before me and that of Abraham, the Friend of the Merciful God."[63]

The Apostle also said, "He who will remember God when he performs his ablution will have his whole body purified by God. But he who will not remember God at his ablution will not have his body purified except in those places where the water was applied."[64] And again, "He who performs the ablution while pure, will be credited with ten good deeds by God."[65] He also said, "An ablution upon ablution is like a light upon light."[66]

All this is to urge and induce men to repeat and renew their ablution. The Apostle also said, "When a Muslim, during the act of ablution, rinses his mouth, the sins leave it; when he blows his nose, they are gone therefrom; when he washes his hands, the sins, even those beneath his finger-nails, are removed; when he washes his head, he rids it of its sins, even those in and behind his ears, when he washes his feet, he cleanses them from sins, even those beneath his toe-nails. Then, and only then, will his going to the mosque and his prayer therein be meritorious.[67] It has also been related that he who is pure has the same reward as he who is fasting.[68] The Apostle also said, "Whoever performs his ablution well, and then lifts his head unto heaven and says, 'I testify that there is no god but

---

63. *Cf. ibid*, Wudu': 24: Ahmad ibn-Hanbal, Taharah:902.

64. Unidentified.

65. Ibn-Majah, Taharah:73.

66. *Cf.* Surah xxiv: 35. The tradition itself seems to be spurious.

67. Ahmad ibn-Hanbal, Taharah:187.

68. Unidentified. *Cf.* Ahmad ibn-Hanbal, Taharah:195.

Allah alone, He hath no associate, and I testify that Muhammad is His servant, the Apostle, the eight gates of Paradise will be flung open before him and he will enter therein through whichever gate he may desire."[69] [122] Said 'Umar "Good ablution drives away Satan from you." Mujahid also said, "He who is able to go to bed purified, remembering God and penitent, let him do so, for souls are brought back to life in the same condition in which they were when taken away."

The Manner of the Major Ablution

The person should place the vessel which contains the water to his right, and repeating the *basmalah*, he should wash his hands, thrice, then perform the act of abstersion, as has been already described, removing off his body whatever impurities it has. He then should perform the ablution of prayer in the manner already described with the exception of the washing of the feet which he should for the time being defer because to wash the feet and then step on the earth [which is not clean] would be waste of water. He then should pour water over his head, thrice over the right side and thrice over the left. He then should rub his body on either side, the front and the back; let the water flow into the interstices of his beard making it reach the base of the hair whether thick or sparse. A woman, however, need not undo her braids unless she is certain that without undoing them the water will not penetrate into the interstices of her hair. The person should not forget those parts of the body which are bent or concealed, but should guard against touching his penis. Shoud he touch his penis, he should perform the act of ablution all over

69. Ahmad ibn-Hanbal, Taharah:203.

again. If, however, he has already performed his ablution before the major ablution (*ghusl*) he need not go through it again.

These then are the rules of ablution (*wudu*) and the major ablution *(ghusl)*. We have discussed those elements in them which are indispensable for the traveller on the path of the hereafter to know and to do. If on special occasions and under unusual circumstances he may need other points besides these, he should refer himself concerning them to the books of jurisprudence.

Of all we have discussed concerning the major ablution two things are obligatory: good intention and the washing of the whole bodv. In the case of ablution [six things] are obligatory: good intentin, washing the face, washing the arms up to the elbows, wiping the head, washing the feet including the heels, and finally the observation of [the above mentioned] order [in the performance of the act of ablution]. [Washing the different members of the body in] uninterrupted succession (*muwalah*), i.e., to commence washing the second member before the first has dried, and the third before the second has and so on], is not obligatory. The major ablution (*ghusl*) is obligatory after four things: after the emission semen, after the two places of circumcision meet together,[70] after menstruation, and after child-birth. Other than these is simply ordained by custom after the usage of the Prophet (*sunnah*), such as the major ablution of the two feasts, al-Fitr and al-Adha, the major ablution of the Friday and the different feasts, the major ablution of the

70. *Ar iltiqa' al-khitanayn*, a euphemism, metonymically denoting the disappearing of the part of the penis that is above, or beyond, the place of circumcision in the vulva of the woman.

ihram,[71] that of the standing on 'Arafah and Muzdalifah, and at entering Makkah. Also performed after the usage of the Prophet are the three major ablutions during the last three days of the pilgrimage (ayyam al-tashiq),[72] the major ablution of the farewell circumambulation (*tawaf-al-wada*), according to some, the major ablution of the unbeliever when he embraces Islam and is under no obligation to perform it by reason of sexual intercourse and the discharge of semen, the insane when he regains his sanity, and the person who has washed a dead body. All these are desirable.

The Manner of Purification with Sand

If, after trying earnestly to find water, a person is unable to secure any, or is prevented by the presence of some beast or obstacle from reaching the water supply, or whenever the water is needed for the quenching of his thirst or that of his companion, or whenever it belongs to someone else who declines to sell any of it except for too high a price, or when the person himself happens to be suffering from a wound or an ailment, and consequently fears that the use of water may result in the infection of the member or in his acute sickness, he should wait until the time for the fulfilment of the ordinance arrives and then proceed to an elevated land the soil of which is pure, fine, and soft so that it is easily blown into dust. There, with his fingers held closely together, he should pat his palms over the sand, and lifting them to his face,

---

71. The *ihram* is the sacred state in which the Muslim performs the major pilgrimage (*Hajj*) and the minor pilgrimage (*'umrah*).

72. These coincide with the eleventh, twelfth and thirteenth days of *Dhu-al-Hijjah*.

he should wipe every part of it once. As he does that he should purpose in his mind the making of prayer permissible. In wiping his face, he is not required to force the dust beneath the hair whether it be sparse or thick. He should, however, make an effort to wipe his whole face with the dust. This can be accomplished with one single stroke, since the width of the face does not exceed that of the two palms. In deciding whether or not he has covered his whole face, his own opinion is sufficient. He then should remove his ring and pat his palms over the sand a second time, during which he should hold his fingers wide apart. Having done this, he should place the back of the fingers of his right hand over the front part of the fingers of his left in such a way that the tips of the fingers of the one hand will not project beyond the edge of the forefinger of the other. His hands in this position, he should then run his left hand over the back of his right forearm up to the elbow. He then should turn over his hand so that the hollow of his left palm rests over the inner side of his right forearm by the elbow and then should run it down towards the wrist and finish by stroking the outer side of his right thumb with the inner of his left. He then should do the same thing for his left arm. After that he should wipe his two palms against each other and pass the fingers of the one hand between those of the other. The purpose of this regulation is to cover both arms completely up to the elbows through a single patting of the palms over the sand. If this proves impossible the person can pat his palms over the sand one or more times. Having fulfilled this and performed the ordained prayer he may proceed to perform any supererogatory prayer he wishes. If he wishes to combine the enactment of two rites he should perform the act of purification with sand (*tayammum*) over again prior to the enactment of the second rite. Thus every ordained rite should be preceded by a single act of *tayammum*.

PART III

On Cleanliness and Cleansing from the External Bodily Growths and Discharges which are of Two Kinds: Discharges (awsakh) and Growths (ajza)

The first kind, namely, the discharges and the wet excretions of the body. These number eight:

1. That which adheres to the hair of the head such as dirt and lice. Cleansing the head from these through washing, combing and the use of ointment for the orderly arrangement of the hair is desirable. The Apostle was wont to anoint and comb his hair once a week. Furthermore, he used to command [his followers] to do the same, saying, "Anoint your hair once a week."[73] He also said, [123] "He who has but one hair [on his head], let him honour it;"[74] i.e. keep it clean from filth. A certain man with dishevelled hair and ruffled beard came one day before the Apostle. On seeing him, the Apostle said, "Has this man no ointment wherewith to hold his hair?"[75]

---

73. *Cf*, al-Tirmidhi, Libas: 22; Abu Dawud, Tarajjul:1.

74. *Cf.* abu-Dawud, Tarajjul:3.

75. Al-Nasa'i Zinah:58.

Then turning to those present he added, "One of you enters the place as though he were a demon."[76]

2. The discharge which collects in the hole of the ear [*i.e.* the ear-wax]. Wiping will remove what is evident of it, while that which collects at the bottom of the canal should be carefully cleansed after emerging from the bath; for too much of that discharge may be harmful to the hearing of the individual.

3. What collects within the nose of the wet thick mucus and sticks to its [inner walls]. It is removed by inhaling and exhaling.

4. The yellow deposits which collect between the teeth and the tip of the tongue. These are removed by the use of the toothpick and the rinsing of the mouth, both of which we have already discussed.

5. The filth which adhere to the beard and the lice which swarms it whenever it is not tended. These can be gotten rid of by washing and combing. Thus we have it in the well-known tradition that the Apostle never parted with his comb, brush, and mirror whether he was at home or on travel.[77] This in fact was the established custom [among] the Arabians. According to a strange tradition, the Prophet was wont to comb his beard twice a day.[78]

---

76. Does not appear in the tradition.

77. *Cf.* ibn-Sa'd, Vol. II, Pt.2. pp.170-71.

78. Unidentified.

His beard was thick[79] and the same was true of that of abu-Bakr.[80]. 'Uthman, on the other hand, had along but thin beard;[81] while 'Ali had a broad and wide beard which spread out across his chest from shoulder to shoulder.[82] In yet a stranger tradition. 'A'ishah said, "Several people gathered outside the gate of the Apostle's house and he went out to meet them. Just before he went out, I saw him gaze, into the water-vessel and fix his hair and beard. Thereupon, I said to him: 'Do you do such a thing O thou the Apostle of God?' To which he replied: 'Yes, for verily God loveth that His servant should adorn himself whenever he goes out to meet his brethren'."[83] The ignorant might think that the Apostle, like other men, attended his hair and beard because of his desire to appear handsome before people. Such an error on the part of the ignorant is like comparing angels to blacksmiths. On the contrary, the Apostle was commanded by God to fulfil a commission and among the duties therein he was expected to exalt himself before man and inspire respect in their hearts so that they might not belittle and despise him, and to embellish his looks in their sight so that they might not slight him not consequently turn away from him, and thereby give the hyprocrites reason to rejoice. Care for personal appearance is obligatory upon every

---

79. See ibn-Sa'd, Vol. I, pt.2, p.120.

80. *Cf. ibid*, Vol.III, Pt.1, p.133.

81. *Ibid*, Vol.III, Pt.2, p.40.

82. *Ibid*, Vol.III, Pt.1, p.16.

83. Unidentfied.

learned man who undertakes to call men to the worship of God. He should attend to his outward appearance so that he would leave nothing that will alienate men and turn them away from him. In this and in other similar things the intention of the individual is the test. For such actions are qualified and coloured by the purpose for which they have been done. Adornment for this purpose is, therefore, desirable; while leaving the beards dishevelled and neglecting one's personal appearance in order to attract attention as an ascetic is extremely dangerous. Rather to relinquish [such affectations] and undertake those things which are more important is desirable. In short, these are inward states between the servant and his God. The critical [observer] will not fall to see that and no amount of ambiguity and confusion could prevail over him or mislead him. Yet how many an ignorant person affects these things in order to attract the attention of men, thereby deceiving himself and other people as well, and claims that his purpose in that is good and wholesome. Thus you often see several learned men wear expensive and luxuriant garments and claim that their sole purpose is to confound heretics and refute dissenters, and that their aim is to draw nigh unto God. But the [falsity of their claim will be reveald on that day when the hearts are examined, when the tombs are laid open and their contents are scattered, when the secret thoughts are made known. On that day will the pure gold be selected and the glittering [brass] thrown away. We seek thy refuge O Lord against the shame [due the hypocrites on the day of judgment].

6. The filth which adheres to the knuckles, *i.e.* the finger joints. These the Arabians did not wash frequently because they neglected the washing of their hands after meals. Consequently, filth collected [124] in these wrinkles. The Apostle of God commanded them, therefore to wash their knuckles.[84]

7. Cleaning the finger-tips which the Apostle of God commanded the Arabians to do.[85] This includes not only the removal of the filth that adheres to the finger-tips but also that which gathers beneath the nails, especially since the nails were not always trimmed, with the result that dirt collected in great quantities beneath them. Consequently, the Apostle ordered that the manicuring of nails plucking the hair off the arm-pits, and shaviing the pubes should be done [at least] once every forty days,[86] but he commanded that the part beneath the nails be cleaned regularly [and frequently].[87] In one of the incidents in the life of the Prophet we are told that he once thought the revelation he was expecting was unduly late; so when finally Gabriel came down with the revelation, the latter said, "How could we reveal to you [anything] when ye wash not your knuckles and clean not your finger-tips when your teeth are yellow and ye clean them not. Command,

---

84. *Cf.* ibn-Majah, Taharah:8; al-Tirmidhi, Adab:14.

85. *Cf.* al-Tirmidhi, Adab:14.

86. *Ibid*, Adab:15.

87. Unidentified.

therefore, your people to do that,"[88] The words of God; "And say not to them, 'Fie!'[89] means not to reproach them for whatever dirt they may have beneath their nails, or, as has also been said, not to be annoyed with them as you are annoyed by the dirt which collects beneath your nails.

8. The dirt which collects to the body through perspiration and dust, all of which are best removed by taking a bath. In this connexion [we may point out that] there is no harm in frequenting the public baths, as the Companions themselves went into the baths of Damascus. One of them even said, "What a good place is the bathhouse! Therein the body is cleansed and its heat reminds us of Hell." This saying has been ascribed to both abu-al-Darda' and abu Ayyub-al-Ansari.[90] Another said, "What a bad place is the bathhouse! Therein nakedness is revealed and shame goes to the winds." The first has addressed himself to the benefits of the bath while

---

88. Unidentified.

89. *Surah* xvii:24.

90. The standard-bearer fo the Porphet. He harboured Muhammad in al-Madinah at the time of al-Hajrah. Later he accompanied Yazid I, then a crown-prince, on his expedition against Constantinople (A.H.49/AD. 669) where he died of dysentery and was buried outside the walls of the Byzantine capital. His tomb became a shrine even to the Christian Greeks who made pilgrimage to it in time of drought to pray for rain. During the siege of Constantinople by the Turks in 1453, the tomb was miraculously discovered by rays of light which shone from it. Thus did the Midnesead gentleman become a saint for three nations. See ibn-Sa'd, Vol.III, Pt.2, pp.49-50; Philip K. Hitti, *History of the Arabs* (London, 1963). pp.201-202.

the second pointed out its evils. At any rate there are certain obligations and rules which the visitor of the bath should observe. Two of these obligations pertain to his own nakedness and two relate to the nakedness of others.

The two obligations which pertain to his own nakedness are first, that he should shield it from the sight of others and second, guard against the touch of others. No one should undertake to clean it but himself. Furthermore, he should not allow the bath attendant who rubs the backs of bathers and massages their body to touch either his thigh or the part of the body which lies between the navel and the pubes. Some permit the touching of any part of the body with the exception of the genitals but the best rule is not to permit the touching of the parts already mentioned, since the rule which prohibits looking at the private parts has been extended to include the prohibition of touching them as well. The same rule covers the other part of nakedness, namely, the thigh.

The two obligations which relate to the nakedness of others are first, to avoid looking at it whenever it is exposed and the second to warn against uncovering it because to warn against evil is obligatory. The person is expected to warn against uncovering the nakedness but he is not held responsible for the acceptance of his warning. He cannot escape the obligation of warning except when such warning exposes him to physical danger or personal injury, or lead him to something which in itself is unlawful. Then he is not expected to condemn one unlawful act when such condemnation will compel the offender to commit another unlawful act. To refrain from warning and excuse himself on the ground that his warning will be of no use is quite unpardonable because no one will fail to take cognizance of disapproval and be influenced by it and no one will fail to take heed when he is derided for his sins. It will result in making the matter seem bad in his sight and will induce him to shun it. For this reason it is not permissible to neglect warning. Consequently, it has become discerete and wise not to frequent the public baths nowadays, because they are always full of exposed nakedness particularly the part of the body extending from the navel to the upper part of the pubes, which part is not considered nakedness by people any more, although the Law has included it therein, and has made it a sort of boundary to nakedness. It is therefore desirable to evacuate the bath-house of people [in return for a certain feel]. In this connexion Bishr ibn-al-Harith said, "I shall not be hard on the man who pays his last dirham in order to have the bath-house evacuated of people when he takes his bat." Ibn-'Umar was once seen in the bath-house with his face turned toward the wall having also blindfolded his eyes with a bandage. Some have said that there was no harm in frequenting the bath-houses provided the individual has two veils, one for covering his nakedness and the other for his head over which he should throw it in order to protect his eyes.

As to the rules, they are ten. They are as follows:

[The first] is good intention. The individual should not enter the bath-house for the sake of some immediate worldly gain or for the purpose of toying with some earthly passion. Rather, he should seek therewith healthy cleanliness in preparation for prayer. [In the second place] he should pay the bath-owner his fee in advance before entering the bath because the service which [the client] wants is unknown to the owner and similarly is the fee which the latter expects. Consequently, the payment of the fee in advance before going into the bath removes [125] the ambiguity from at least the one and sets the mind of the other at ease.

[In the third place], the individual should advance his left foot first as he enters the bath and should then say, "In the name of God the Merciful, the Compassionate. I seek refuge in God against Satan, the accursed' the filthy, the impure, the corrupt, the corrupting." [Fourthly], he should await the time when the bath is vacant and then go in, or see to it, by paying, that it is vacated. For although there may not be in the bath any except religious men who are careful not to expose their nakedness, the very fact of seeing their unprotected bodies smacks of lack of shame and is suggestive of nakedness. Furthermore, it is unavoidable in moving about not to expose the nakedness especially as the flaps of the veil turn and fold. Then the individual cannot help but see the nakedness of others. It was for this reason that ibn-'Umar blindfolded his eyes [whenever he entered a bath-house].

[In the fifth place], the individual should wash his hands as he enters the bath. [Sixthly], he should not rush into the tank room until he had first been through the first room [where men sit to perspire]. [Seventhly], he should not use too much water but should limit himself to no more than he needs as the occasion demands. To go beyond that will offend the bath-owner especially when the wasted water is hot which costs money and requires labour.

[Eighth], the heat of the bath-house should remind the individual of the heat of Hell and, having spent one hour in the heat of the bath-house, he should try to get an idea of [the endless stay of sinners in] Hell. It is the place most like Hẹll, both in the fire beneath the water and the darkness above. We seek refuge in God against all such things.

As a matter of fact, the wise will not fail to remember the hereafter every moment of his life, because it is his final destination and eternal abode. In everything he sees, whether it be water, or fire, or any other thing, he finds warning and admonition. For every man notices the things most familiar to himself. Thus if a dry-goods man, a carpenter, a mason, and a weaver entered a furnished house, you would find, on examination, that the dry-goods man looks at the draperies and scrutinises their value; the weaver directs his attention to the clothes and examines their textures; the carpenter gazes at the ceiling and ponders over its construction; and the mason turns to the walls and deliberates over the manner of their building and the exactness of their lines. Similarly, the traveller on the road of the hereafter does not see anything without finding in it a lesson as well as a reminder of the hereafter. In fact, his eyes fall on nothing without receiving from God a warning. If he sees something black he remembers the darkness of the grave; if he sees a snake he is reminded of the serpents of Hell; if he sees any ugly face the image of Munkar and Nakir as well as that of the tormenting angels (*al-zabaniya*)[91] appear before him; if he hears a terrific noise his mind turns to the blowing of the horn on the Last Day; if he sees something beautiful he recalls the bliss of Paradise and if he hears someone say 'yes' or 'no' in the market-place or in a house he reverts in his thoughts to his own fate on the day of judgment, whether he will be accepted or rejected. How becoming it is, then, that such things should prevail over the heart of the wise. Nothing dissuades him therefrom except the most important matters of life. But if he should compare the length of his stay in this life with that of his abode in the hereafter, he would despise the former if he were mindful and wise.

[The ninth] of these rules is that the individual should not salute [the bystanders] on entering the bath-house, and in case he was saluted he should not return the salutation. If he should feel inclined to reply to the salutation he may do so by saying

---

91. Certain angels whose duty is to thrust the people of Hell into the fires thereof. *Cf. Surah* lxvi:6.

"May God forgive you your sins."[92] He may shake hands with [an acquaintance bystander] and, for the sake of commencing a conversation, say, "May God forgive you your sins"; but this conversation should not be prolonged. Furthermore, he should not repeat the Qur'an in the bath-house except in his mind, yet there is no harm in repeating aloud the formula. "I seek refuge in God against Satan, the accursed." Again the practice of going into the bath-house between the hour of sunset and nightfall (al-isha'an) is undesirable, because at that time the demons roam [the earth].

The bather may have someone else to rub his back and massage his body for him, as it has been related that Yusuf ibn—Asbat has, before he died, requested that a certain stranger be allowed to wash his corpse after his death and said, "The man has rubbed my back and massaged my body for me when I was once bathing, I wish therefore to reward him with something which will please him, and I am sure it will please him much to wash my corpse." The permissibility of having another rub one's back and massage his body is attested by what one of the Companions related concerning the Apostle of God. Said the Companion, "In one of his travels the Apostle of God stopped at an inn. Stretching himself out with his belly to the earth, a negro slave began to massage his back for him. Therefore, I said,

92. The individual may reply to a salutation in the bath with the words *'afah Allah* but never with the usual formlaa of *wa-'alay-kum al-slam wa rahmat Allah*.

'What is going on O Apostle of God?' To which he replied, "The she-camel threw me off its back."

Finally, when the individual is through with his bathing he should thank God upon this blessing, for it has been said that hot water in winter time is a much sought of luxury. Concerning baths and bathing ibn-'Umar said, "Baths are an innovated luxury." This describes baths in their relation to the Law, but from the view-point of medicine they have been described as a protection against leprosy, especially after the use of a depilatory. It has also been said that depilating the pubes once a month cools the body, purifies the complexion, and increases virility.

Again it has been said, "To urinate while standing in the bath in winter time is better for the man than a dose of medicine." And again "To sleep after the bath in the summer time is as good as any dose of medicine. "Washing the feet with cold water after the bath is a protection against gout. Furthermore, the pouring of cold water over the head, as well as drinking it, after the bath is undesirable. These rules [govern the conduct] of men [in bath houses].

As to women the Apostle said, "It is not lawful unto a man to take his wife into a bath-house when others are bathing therein."[93] According to a tradition vouched for by more than two Companions (mashhur), "It is unlawful for the man to enter the bath-house without a veil, and it is

93. *Cf.* al-Tirmidhi, Adab:43.

unlawful for the woman to enter [126] therein except after childbirth or when sick."[94] 'A'ishah herself entered the bath-house when she was sick. Thus whenever the woman has to go into the bath-house let her do so veiled. It is undesirable for the man to give her the fee lest it be a help for her to do that which is undesirable.

The second kind is bodily growths and falls into eight groups

The first is the hair of the head in the shaving of which there is no harm to him who desires to be clean. On the other hand there is no harm in leaving it grow provided it is regularly anointed and combed, and provided it is not left to grow in tufts as the smart set are wont to do, or in long locks like the manner of the descendants of the noble blood (ahl al-sharaf)[95] to whom the practice has become a distinctive sign. Unless the person be a descendant of noble blood his wearing of long locks would be false and fake.

The second is the hair of the moustache. The Apostle said, "Cut your moustaches off." According to another version, "Shear your moustaches." And according to another, "Trim your moustaches and spare your beard."[96] In other words let your moustaches extend around the upper lip [but not

94. Ibn-Majah Adab:38.

95. Namely, the descendants of 'Ali, more particularly through al-Hasan.

96. *Cf.* Muslim, Taharah:67-70; al-Bukhari, Libas;66; al-Tirmidhi, Adab:18.

hang down over it], i.e. let them encircle it. Of the same root is the phrase "circling round" in the verse, "And thou shalt see the angels circling round about the throne."[97] In still another version the word used is "pluck"[98] which indicates cutting extremely short while "trim" indicates a lesser extent. Said God, "Should He ask them of you and press you, you would show yourselves niggards."[99] In other words "should He urge you."

Shaving the moustache, however, was never mentioned in the tradition, while trimming so closely as to resemble shaving has been related about thẹ Companions. Thus one of the followers (al-tabi'un), on seeing a person who had trimmed his moustache very closely, said, "You remind me of the Companions of the Apostel of God." Al-Mughirah ibn-Shu'bah[100] once said, "One day the Apostle of God saw me with a long moustache. There upon he said, come hither and have your moustache cut off along a toothpic."[101] There is, however, no harm in leaving its extremities (i.e. its ends) to hang down. 'Umar and thers besides him did that, because the ends of the moustache do not cover the

---

97. *Surah* xxxxi:75.

98. Al-Nasa'i, Taharah:14.

99. *Surah* xlvii:39.

100. A Companion who was appointed governor of Al-Basrah by 'Umar who later appointed him governor of al-Kufah. 'Uthamn removed him from the governorship of al-Kufah is which Mu'awiyah reinstated him. He died A.H. 50/A.D. 670. See on Sa'd Vol.IV p.2, pp.24-26, Vol. VI, p.12; ibn-Qutaybah, pp. 50,51.

101. Al-Tayalisi:698.

mouth and no food sticks to them while eating. The words of the Apostle, "Spare the beards," mean let them grow. According to one tradition the Apostle said, "The Jews spare their moustache and trim their beards; but ye do the opposite."[102] Some learned men disapproved of shaving and regarded it an innovation.

The third is the hair growth on the armpit the plucking of which is desirable at least once every forty days. Such an operation is quite easy and simple at the person has been accustomed to it right from the beginning. But the person who has been accustomed to remove it by shaving may continue to do, so especially since its plucking is tormenting and painful while the sole purpose of its removal is cleanliness and the prevention of dirt from collecting in the interstices of the hair. This purpose is equally attained through shaving.

The fourth is the hair on the pubes, the removal of which is desirable either by shaving or by the use of a depilatory. Its removal should not be delayed any longer than forty days.

Fifth are the nails, the manicuring of which is desirable especially because of their horrible appearance and because of the dirt which collects underneath them when they are long. The Apostle of God said, "O Abu-Hurayrah, inanicure your nails for Satan sitteth on them when they are long."[103] The presence of a little dirt underneath the nails

102. *Cf.* al-Bukhari, Libas: 64; Muslim, Taharah: 67-70.

103. Unidentified.

will not effect the validity of ablution, because such little dirt will not prevent the water from penetrating [underneath the nails]. Furthermore because of necessity, both the Bedouins and the city people are usually lenient in this matter, particularly in connexion with the toe-nails, the knuckles, and the back of the feet and the hands. The Apostle of God was wont to command [his followers] to manicure their nails and take them to task for the dirt underneath their nails. But he did not command them to repeat their prayer. If he had done so his commandment would have had the added benefit of admonishment and warning against [uncleanliness].

Concerning the manner of manicuring the nails, I have not seen any genuine tradition. But I have heard that the Apostle of God, when manicuring his nails, began with the index finger of the right hand and finished with the thumb.[104] [Starting with the index finger of the right hand, he worked to the little finger of the same hand]. Moving then to the left hand he worked from the little finger to the thumb. [Last of all he manicured the thumb of the right hand]. Pondering over this, one of its aspects, which seems to prove its veracity, occurred to me. Now such things do not become apparent except through the light of prophecy. But learned men of insight [127] aim at deducing through reasoning the significance of these things when reported to them. What occurred to me, although God knows best, is that manicuring the nails of the fingers and toes is,

---

104. No such tradition is found.

to begin with necessary. But whereas the hand is superior to the foot, a person should begin with the fingers. Of the two hands, the right is the superior and consequently should come first. Of the five fingers of the right hand the index finger, which points out [at people] when one is repeating the two words of the *Shahadah*, is the superior. Therefore, it should mark the beginning. Since the order favoured by the Law in matters of ablution and the like is to begin with the right and proceed in the same direction, the finger to the right of the index should come next. If the hand is placed with its back to the ground then the thumb would be the finger to the right of the index. If it is placed with its palm to the ground then the middle finger would be to the right of the index. But if you let the hand dangle naturally, its palm would be inclined towards the ground because the right hand swings from the right to the left, and as the swinging motion is completed the back of the hand goes up. Hence the natural position is the more preferable. Furthermore, if one palm is placed against the other the fingers form, as it were, a circle, and consequently the person should commence with the index finger of the right hand and from there work to the right until he returns to the same index finger. This will result in working from the index finger of the right to the little finger of the same hand, and then from the little finger of the left hand to the thumb of the same hand. There remains the thumb of the right hand, with which the operation should be concluded.

As to the toes, since no tradition governing the procedure of manicuring them has come down to us, I hold it to be better to being with little toe of the right foot and, working to the right, end with the little toe of the left foot, which is exactly like procedure followed in cleaning between the toes.[105] For the considerations which we have mentioned in connexion with the hands do not hold here since there is no "fore-finger," [that points out at people when one repeats the two words of the *shahadah*] in the foot. In fact, all the toes are in the same category and form a single line close to the ground. Therefore, one begins with the right. Nevertheless any such assumption of their forming, as it were, a circle when the sole of the one foot is placed against that of the other, unlike the same thing in the case of the fingers, is unnatural. These minute details of procedure become instantly apparent through the light of prophecy, but in our case they are extremely difficult.

If we were asked concerning the order of procedure [which should be followed in manicuring the nails] we might be able to give a satisfactory reply; but if we cite the practice of the Apostle of God and the procedure which he followed therein, we might be able thereby to ascertain its rule. His reminder [to us through his practice] of the significance [of his procedure therein] calls for the deduction of that significance. No one should think that the actions of the Apostle, and all their details, have not been governed by a definite standard, and

105. See above, pp.43-44.

a fixed rule and order. In fact in all the voluntary actions which we have already mentioned man follows one of two or more procedures, the selection of which is motivated not by sheer agreement but by a definite reason which demands that procedure be followed and preferred. For the haphazard way of doing things just as they come is characteristic of animals; while governing actions and movements by the standard of their [relative] significance is peculiar of the saints of God. The more regulated and governed are the actions and movements of man, and the less they are haphazard and neglected and the farther removed they are from [caprice], the nearest would his rank be to that of the prophets and saints and the closer would his position be to God. This is because he who is close to the Prophet is close to God. Furthermore, he who is close to God is, in the nature of the case, one of His favourites, and he who stands close to the favourite is in turn a favourite. We, therefore, seek refuge in God against having the direction of our actions and movements in the hands of Satan, ruled and governed by him through [our] passions and whims.

The manner in which the Apostle applied kohl to his eyes has been accepted as the norm and standard for such procedures. He was wont to apply it thrice to the right and twice to the left eye beginning with the right for its superiority. The disparity between the number of applications to each eye is for the sake of having the sum total odd in number,[106] because odd numbers are superior to

---

106. *Cf.* ibn Majah, Taharah:23.

even numbers. God himself is unique and prefers odd [numbers]. Consequently, the actions of man should always correspond to one of the attributes of God. For this reason the use of an odd number of stones in abstersion has been viewed with favour. The number of the applications of kohl to the eyes has not been limited to three, although there is an odd number, because the share of the left eye would then be one application only, which thing in insufficiant and will not ordinarily extend over all the roofs of the eyelashes. The right eye has been assigned three applications because preference is necessary to produce an uneven number, and since the right eye is superior it enjoys that preference.

If you should say, "Why was the left eye limited to two applications?" my answer would be that the limitation was dictated by necessity, since if each eye were given an odd number of applications the sum total of the applications would be even, because the sum of two odd numbers is an even number. But the preference if for an odd number in the total applications of both eyes rather than of each eye. There is, however, another possibility in the applications of kohl, namely to follow the practice in ablution and apply the kohl thrice to each eye.[107] This procedure is the more preferable. If I were to investigate all the details which the Prophet observed in his actions and movements, it will take me a long long time to exhaust the subject. Therefore, base your future in your past experience; and know that no learned man will ever become the

107. Al-Tirmidhi, Libas:23.

heir of the Prophet unless he acquaints himself with all the statutes of the Law, so that nothing will separate them [*i.e.* learned man, and Prophet] from each other [128] except one rank—that of prophecy which is the distinguishing degree between the inheritor and the inherited. For the inherited is he who has earned and collected the money while the inheritor is he who has neither earned nor collected is but received it by transmission. These and other significations, despite their relative easiness when compared with the profound mysteries and secrets, are not independently comprehended except by the Prophets and are not elicitied through transmission, after their [importance] has been pointed out by the prophets, except by their heirs, the learned men.

The sixth and seventh are the navel cord and the foreskin respectively. The navel cord is cut off at the time of birth while purification through circumcision is performed by the Jews on the seventh day after birth; consequently, contradicting them by delaying the operation until the child cuts his front teeth is more desirable and less dangerous. The Apostle said "Circumcision is a law unto man and a meritorious deed on the part of women.'[108] Nevertheless, excess should be avoided in female circumcision. The Apostle once said to umm 'Atiyah[109] who used to practise the circumcision of women, "O umm-'Atiyah! Be moderate when you perform the operation of

---

108. Unidentified.

109. One of the women Companions of the Prophet. See ibn Sa'd Vol.8, pp. 333-34

circumcision on women and cut off only a small portion of the prepuce of the clitoris, for that is better fitted to preserve feminity and more welcome to masculinity."[110] In other words it does not impair the woman's passion nor rob the man of his pleasure at the time of intercourse. Behold them the refined diction and euphemism of the Apostle's speech and how the light of prophecy has shone from the affairs of the hereafter which are the noblest concerns of prophecy and illuminated the affairs of this world do that matters of great importance, the ignorance of which may result in grave, consequences, have been revealed to the Apostle despite the fact that he was unlettered (*ummi*) Praise, therefore, be to God who has sent His Apostle to be a mercy unto men and through him to make available for them the blessings of this world and of the world to come.

The eighth is the long beard the discussion of which we deferred in order to append to it certain rules which govern it and several innovations practised in connexion with it, since this is the most suitable place for the treatment. People have differed as to the length of the beard. Some held that there is no harm in the person taking his beard with his hand and cutting off what projects below his grip. This was done by ibn-'Umar and several of the followers (al-tabi'un) and met the approval of al-Shu'bi and ibn-Sirin but was frowned at by al-Hasan

---

110. Abu-Dawud, Adab:167.

[al-Basri] and Qafadah[111] who said that letting it alone is a better practice, which conforms to the words of the Prophet, "Spare your beards."[112] The right practice is not difficult to determine, provided it does not lead to trimming the beard and rounding it off the sides; for its excessive length renders the appearance unseemly and releases the tongues of backbiters with ridicule. Consequently, it is better to avoid such practice. Al-Nakha'i said, "I wonder why a sane man whose beard is long does not trim it, thereby avoiding its being too long and its being too short, for moderation is desirable and good in everything." For this reason it has been said, "The bigger the beard the smaller the mind."

There are, in connexion with the beard, ten disapproved practices. Of these some are more reprehensible than the others. These are dyeing the beard black, bleaching it with sulphur, plucking it, plucking the gray hairs in it, [elaborately] trimming it augmenting its size, neglecting it, dishevelled and untidy for the sake of affecting asceticism, boasting of its black colour as indicative of youth and of its gray colour as the sign of [venerable] age, and dyeing it red or yellow, thereby emulating the righteous but lacking [their good] intention.

The first [disapproved practice] in connexion with the beard is dyeing it black. The practice is forbidden as the Apostle said concerning it, "The

---

111. Ibn-Diamah al-Sadhasi, A.H. 117/A.D. 735. See ibn-Sa'd, Vol.VII, Pt.2, pp.1-3; ibn-Qutaybah, pp. 234-35.

112. See above, p. 73.

best of your youth are those who emulate the old among you, and the worst of your old men are those who emulate the youthful among you."[113] Emulating the old refers to the emulation of their poise and dignity not their gray hair. Not only was the dyeing of the hair black forbidden[114] but it was also described as the sign of the people of Hell, and according to another version it was identified with the sign of the unbelievers.[115]

A certain man who was living at the time of 'Umar and was wont to dye his beard black got married. Soon afterwards the dye faded and his gray hair was no longer concealed. Thereupon the relatives of his wife brought him before the Caliph who annulled his marriage and had him flogged, and said to him, "You deceived them by concealing from them your gray hair."

It is said that the first to dye his beard black was Pharaoh, may the curse of God be upon him. It is also related on the authority of ibn-'Abbas that the Prophet said, "At the end of time there will be [129] men who will dye their beards black like the crop of the pigeon; the same will not enjoy the fragrance of Paradiise."[116]

The second [practice] is dyeing the beard yellow or red. The practice is permissible in order to

---

113. Unidentified and probably spurious.

114. Abu-Dawud, Tarajjul: 18; al-Nasa'i Zinah;15.

115. Neither tradition is identified.

116. Abu-Dawud. Tarajjul; 20; al-Nasa'i Zinah:15.

conceal the age of warriors from the unbelievers in times of raids and Jihad. If it is not for this purpose but rather for the sake of emulating men of religion, then it is blameworthy. The Apostle of God said, "Yellow is the colour with which the Muslims dye their beards, and red is that with which the believers dye theirs."[117] Henna was used for red dye while saffron and phillyrea for the yellow.

Some of the learned men dyed their beards black before setting out on raids. There is no harm in this practice provided the intention is genuine and is not shadowed by passion or lust.

The third [practice] is bleaching the beard with sulphur to give the appearance of an advanced age for the purpose of gaining deference and veneration having their testimony accepted at court and their narration of traditions on the authority of the masters accredited; they do it out of their desire to lord it over youth and in order to appear very learned, thinking that age would make them superior. But how far from the truth this is; for age does not increase the ignorance except with ignorance. Knowledge is the fruit of reason which is a native talent removed from the influence of age and not affected by gray hair. But he who is born foolish increases in folly with the years. Furthermore, the masters (*al-shuyukh*) were wont to give precedence to the learned youths. Thus 'Umar used to give ibn-'Abbas, despite his youth, precedence over the leading Companions, and used

---

117. Unidentified.

to seek his counsel rather than theirs. Ibn-'Abbas himself said, "God giveth not His servants knowledge except in their youth and in youth lieth all that is good." In support of his assertion he cited the words of God when He said, "They said, 'We heard a youth make mention of them: They call him Abraham."[118] He also cited the words of God, "They were youths who had believed in their Lord, and in guidance had We increased them;"[119] and also, "And We bestowed on him wisdom while yet a child."[120]

Anas was wont to say, "The Apostle of God died having in his head and beard no more than twenty gray hairs." On being told, "But abu-Hamzah! The Apostle was well advanced in age when he died," Anas replied, "Yes. But God did not disgrace him with gray hair?" "Is is a disgrace to have gray hair?" they asked. Anas replied, "Do you not all dislike gray hair?"[121].

It is also said that Yahya ibn-Aktham[122] was appointed judge when he was twenty-one years old. While sitting in his court one day a certain man, wishing to deride him for his young years, asked him, "Of what age is the judge, may God establish

---

118. *Surah* xxi:61.

119. *Surah* xviii:12.

120. *Surah* xix:13.

121. *Cf.* ibn-Sa'd Vol.I, Pt.2, pp.135-39.

122. Abu Muhammad ul-Tamimi al-Morwazi, A.H. 249/A.D. 857. He was the judge of al-Basrah and later the chief judge of Baghdad under al-Ma'mun, See ibn-Khallikan, Vol.III, pp.175-187; al-Baghdadi, Vol.X, IV, pp.191-204.

him?". Ibn-Aktham retorted, "Of the same age as 'Attab ibn-Aaidi[123] when the Apostle of God entrusted him with the governorship of Makkah and its judgeship," and with this retort silenced him. It was also reported on the authority of Malik that he said, "I read in one of the books the following statement, 'Let not a man's beard deceive you for the bull has one also!'".

Abu-'Amr ibn-al-'Ala[124] said, "Whenever you see that a man is tall in stature but his head is small and beard long and wide be sure that he is a fool although he may be Umayyah ibn-'Abd-Shams."[125] Ayyub al-Sakhtiyani[126] said, "I have seen old men of eighty years follow a youth in order to learn from him." Ali-Ibn al-Husayn[127] said, "He who has preceded you in knowledge is your Imam in this respect though he may be younger than you in years."

---

123. Governor of Makkah under the Prophet. He died A.H., 13 A/D. 634. See ibn-Sa'd. Vol. V, p.330; ibn-Qutaybah, p.144; *Tahdhib al-Asma*, p.445.

124. One of the seven Qur'an readers, died A.H. 154 A.H. 771. see *al-Fihrist*, p.28; ibn-Khallikan, Vol II, 105-8.

125. Famous ancestor of the Umayyads and most noble scion of the Quraysh. See ibn-Durayd al-Azd *Kitab al-Ishtiqaq*, ed. F. Wustenfeld (Cottengen, 1854), p.103.

126. A.H. 131 A.D. 748-49, See ibn-Qutaybah, pp.234-39; al-Sam'ani, f 291, b; *Tahdhib al-Asma'*, pp.170-71

127. Grandson of 'Ali ibn-abi-Talib, known as Zayn-al-Abidin, A.H. 94/A.D. 713. See ibn-Qutaybah, pp.100-11; ibn Sa'd, Vol. V, pp.156-65; ibn Khallikan, Vol.I, pp.575-77.

Abu-'Amr ibn-al-'Ala was once asked, is it becoming to the old man to learn from youth?" He answered saying, "Ignorance abases man and knowledge ennobles him." Yahya ibn-Mu'in, on seeing Ahmad ibn-Hanbal walking behind a mule ridden by al-Shafi'i told him "O abu-'Abdullah, I see that you have discontinued the company of Sufyan,[128] despite his advanced age, for the company of this youth in order to learn for him." Ahmad replied, "If you only knew [what is good] you would have walked behind his mule from the other side. If, because of his death, I should miss receiving the knowledge of Sufyan from him personally, I could get it at anytime through other transmitters. But if I should miss the company of this youth I would never receive any of his learning either directly from him or indirectly through [transmitters]."

The fourth practice is plucking the gray hairs of the beard because of one's loathing for gray hair. The Apostle of God has definitely forbade the plucking of gray hair and said that it was the light of the believer.[129] It is of the same nature as dyeing the hair black and the reasons of its being disapproved have already been mentioned. Gray hair is the light of God and he who dislikes it dislikes the light.

The fifth practice is plucking the beard in whole or in part for fun or play. This is disapproved—it

---

128. Probably ibn-'Uyaynah' rather than al-Thawri since the later died three years before ibn-Hambal was born.

129. *Cf.* al-Tirmidhi, Fada'il al-Jihad: 9; al-Nasa'i, Jihad: 25.

renders the appearance unseemly. Similarly, plucking the hair off either side of his lower lips is an innovation. A certain man who was wont to pluck the hair off the side of the lower lip took the witness stand before 'Umar ibn-'Abd-al-'Aziz [133] but [the caliph] rejected his testimony. Likewise, 'Umar ibn-al-Khattab and ibn-abi-Layla,[130] the judge of al-Madinah refused to accept the testimony of any person whose practice it was to pluck his beard.

Plucking the beard during its early growth in order to appear beardless is among the major evils. For the beard is the ornament of man. Furthermore, there are among the angels of God some who swear saying, "By Him who hath adorned mankind with beards." It is one of the signs of perfect creation and distinguishes men from women. According to [some] singular interpretation *(Gharib al-ta'wil)* it is the beard which is meant by the words of God which He said, "He addeth to His creatures what He will"[131] The followers of al-Ahnaf ibn-Qays remonstrated saying, "We wish we could purchase for al-Ahnaf a beard though it may cost us twenty thousand."[132]

---

130. A.H. 148/A.D. 765. He was judge of al-Madinah under the Umayyads and later became judge of al-Kufah under the 'Abbasids. See ibn-Sa'd, Vol, VI, p.249; ibn-Qutaybah, p.248.

131. *Surah* xxxv: 1.

132. Al-Ahnaf was bow-legged and one-eyed as well as beardless. *cf.* ibn-Qutaybah, pp.216-17; ibn-Khallikan, Vol.I, pp, 411-15.

Shurayh al-Qadi[133] said, "I wish I had a beard though it were for ten thousand." For how could the beard be disliked when it gives the man honour, identifies him in the sight of others with learning, induces them to look up to him with respect, gives him the exalted seat in the assemblies [of the learned], focuses the eyes of all upon him, entitles him to precedence over his associates, and shields him from dishonour, since he who curses is restrained from it if the man has a beard? It is said that all the inhabitants of Paradise are beardless except Aaron, the brother of Moses, who has a beard which reaches down to his navel. It has been given him as a special favour and distinction.

The sixth practice is trimming the beard in successive contours for the sake of attracting women. Said Kab', "There will be at the end of time men who will trim their beards in the shape of the dove-tail, and will have the toes of their shoes upturned like a scythe. Such people have no manners."

The seventh practice is augmenting the size of the beard by allowing the hair which covers the temples, which belongs to the head, to grow and join that of the said whiskers thereby going beyond the limits of the ordinary beard and reaching halfway down the cheeks. This is contrary to the habit becoming the righteous.

---

133. So called because he was the incumbent judge of al-Kufah, to which office he was appointed by 'Umar. He died A.H. 78 or 79/A.D. 698. See ibn-Qutaybah, p.221; *Tahdhib al-Asma'*, pp.313-14.

The eighth practice is combing the beard for the sake [of attracting the attention] of men. Bishr[134] said concerning beards, "There are two sins in connexion with beards: combing them for the sake of [attracting the attention of] men and neglecting them dishevelled to appear before them ascetic.

The ninth and tenth practices are respectively to admire the beard's blackness and its grayness. Such self-admiration is blame-worthy with regard to all the members of the body as well as traits and actions, as will later be discussed.

This is what we have intended to discuss of the various kind of adornment and cleanliness. Three traditions dealing with the rules which govern the body have given us twelve items of which five pertain to the head, namely parting the hair, rinsing the mouth, inhaling and exhaling water [for cleaning the nose], trimming the moustache, and using the toothpick; three pertain to the hands, namely manicuring the nails, washing the knuckles, and cleaning the finger-tips; and four pertain to the body, namely plucking the hair of the arm-pits, shaving the pubes, circumcision, and abstersion with water—all of which have been mentioned in tradition.[135]

Now whereas the purpose of this book is to discuss outward and physical cleanliness rather

---

134. Perhaps Bishr ibn-al-Harith al-Hafi, A.H. 227 A. D. 841. See ibn-Qutaybah, p.261; al-Sha'rani Vol, I, pp.62-63.

135. *Cf.* Muslim, Taharah: 49-51; ibn-Majah Taharah:8, al-Tirmidhi, Adab: 14, 15.

than the inward we shall confine ourselves to the former. Let it, however, be known that the inward filth and dirt from which it is necessary to clean oneself are innumberable and we shall take them up in detail in the Quarter on The Destructive Marters of Life and shall also discuss the manner of their removal and the method of purifying the heart therefrom.

Here ends the Book on the Mysteries of Purity, to be followed by that on the Mysteries of Prayer.

LIST OF REFERENCES

Bukhari, al-, *Sahih*, Bulq 1296.

Darimi, al-, *Sunan*, Damascus 1349.

Dawud, abu, *Sunan*, Cairo 1280.

Dhahabi, al-, *Tadhkirat at-Huffaz*, Hyderabad 1333.

Hanbal, Ahmad ibn-, *Musnad*, Cairo 1329-1333.

Majah, ibn-, *Sunan*, Cairo 1349.

Muslim, *Sahih*, Delhi 1319.

Nasa'i, al-, *al-Mujtaba*, Delhi 1315.

Nawawi, al-, *Tahdhib al-Asma,'* ed F. Wustenfeld, Gottingen 1842-1847.

Qutaybah, ibn-, *Kitab al-Ma'arif*, ed. F. Wustenfeld, Gottingen 1850.

Tayalisi, al-, *Musnad*, Hyderabad 1321.

Tirmidhi al-, *Sunan*, Cairo 1920.

Sa'd, ibn-, *Kitab al-Tabaqat al-Kubra*, ed., F. Sachau and others, Leyden 1905-1921.

Sha'rani, al-, *al-Tabaqat al-Kubra*, Cairo 1345.

Yaqut *Mu'jam al-Buldan* ed. F. Wustenfeld, Leipzig 1866-1870.

INDEX OF PROPER NAME

'Abbas, Abdullah ibn-, 30, 69, 70, 71.
Abraham, 39, 71.
Ahnaf, al-, 41.
'A'ishah,24, 36, 47, 58.
Aktham, ibn-, see Yahya ibn-Aktham.
'Ala', abu-'Amr ibn-al-, 72, 73.
'Ali ibn-abi-Talib, 30, 47.
'Ali ibn-al-Hussayn, see Husayn, 'Ali ibn-al-,
Anas ibn-Malik, 71.
Ansari, abu-Ayyub al-, 50.
Arabians, 46, 49.
'Arafah, 42.
Asbat, Yusuf ibn-, see 'Attab ibn Asid.
'Atiyah, umm-, 66.
'Attab ibn-Aaidi, 72.
Ayyub, al-, see Ansari, abu Ayyub al-,
Basri, Hassan al-, 67, 68.
Bishr ibn-al-Harith, 52, 76.
Damascus, 50.
Gabriel, 6.
Hanbal, Ahmad ibn-, 73.
Hudhayafah, 24.
Hurayrah, abu-, 5, 37, 60
Husayn, 'Ali ibn-al-, 72
Ibrahim ibn-Adham, 36.
Ka'b al-Ahbar, 75
Khattab, 'Umar ibn-al-, 4, 5, 16, 24, 40, 69, 70, 74.
Layla, ibn-al-, 74.
Madinah, al-, 15, 74.
Makkah, 15, 72.
Malik ibn-Anas, 15.
Malikites,
Moses, 75.
Mubarak, ibn-al-, 25
Mu'in, Yahya ibn-, 73.
Mujahid, 40
Munkar, 55
Muzdalifah, 42.
Nakha'i, Ibrahim ibn-Yazid al-, 6, 68.
Nakir, 55.
Qa'adah, 68.
Qays, al-Ahnaf ibn-, 74
Quba', 29.
Sa'id ibn-al-Mussayyab, 36.
Sakhtiyan Ayyub al-, 72
Salman al-Farisi, 26
Shafi'i, al-, 14, 15, 16, 73
Shu'bah, 37.
Shu'bah, al-Mughirah ibn-, 59.
Shu'bi, al-, 67.
Shurayah al-Qadi, 75.
Siddiq, Abu-Bakr al-, 47
Sirin, ibn-, 67.
Sufis, 7.
Sufyan ibn-, Uyaynah, 73.
Ta'i, Dawud ibn-Nuṣayr al-, 9.
Thawri, Sufyan al-, 10.
'Umar 'Abdullah ibn-, 13, 37, 52, 53, 57, 67.
'Umar ibn-, Abd-al-' Aziz, 74.
Umayyah ibn-'Abd-Shams, 72.
'Uthman ibn-'Affan, 47.
Yahya ibn-Aktham, 71, 72.
Zuhri, al-, 36.

INDEX OF ARABIC TEXT

ahdath, 23.
ahl al-Sharaf, 58.
ahl al-Suffah, 5.
ajza', 45.
arak, 30.
'awrah, 23.
awsakh, 45.
a'yan, 12.
'ayniyah, 21.
ayyam al-tashri, 42.
fadalat, 2 n
gharib al-ta'wil, 74.
ghusl, 23, 41.
hukmiyah, 21.
ihram, 42.
iltiqa', al-Khitanayn, 41n.
'isha'an, al-, 56.
istinja', 23.
mashhur, 57.
muwalah, 41.
*muzal, al-*12.
muzal bihi, al-, 14.
ru'unah, 7.
sarih, 16.
shahdah, al-, 62, 63.
shuyukh, al-, 70.
sirr, 2.
sunnah, 41.
tabi'un, al-, 67.
takbir, 5.
tawaf al-wada', 42.
tayammum, 23, 55.
ummi, 67.
'umrah, 42 n.
ushnan, 5.
wudu, 23, 41.
zabaniyah, al-, 55.